*the Evidence of Things not Seen...*

by ADÁL

introduction by Victor Hernández Cruz

published for Foto
Da Capo .. New York .. 1975

*Library of Congress Cataloging in Publication Data*

*Adál, 1948–*
  *The evidence of things not seen . . .*

  *1. Photography, Artistic. I. Title.*
*TR654.A3          779'.092'4          74-31350*
*ISBN 0-306-70722-5*
*ISBN 0-306-80013-6 pbk.*

*Printed by Rapoport Printing Corporation*
*Binding by A. Horowitz & Son*

*Published by Da Capo Press, Inc.*
*A subsidiary of Plenum Publishing Corporation*
*227 West 17th Street, New York, N.Y. 10011*

the Evidence of Things not Seen...

*introduction..*

click..

all your life you keep searching for your origins. You drag yourself into the world to drag the world out. To invent your own world is to be free from the chains that hold you to the not so free world. To invent the world is to have the fullest realization of it. Everything that surrounds us has invented itself through some kind of fusion...through some kind of harmony we are all here. Adal has a whole

Set of keys to doors that open to vast regions which
he is beginning to chart. His world is not the unreal world
of fact finders and social realists; his world is the
real world. His work is the experiencing of the fullest potentials of the human senses, primarily vision,
seeing ourselves in our actual light. We are only here
for a little while, we must open as many doors as we can

We have to keep trying to catch up with that original wave of creation and learn how to move like-it for it may be the only way out of here. The best of visual art is the capturing of that force which is its actual invention.. jumping on the movement of everything, walking away from ourselves and not moving an inch catching an object off guard and diving deep into its essence to admire all its magnificence. It is what is actually happening around us— The turning inside out of the mind. Your body becomes your mind and your mind your body. The World is Suspended for a second of the camera click..

— Victor Hernández Crúz

the Evidence of Things not Seen ..

If you come across a grill on the pavement and see your shadow cast into it, then tell me that the shadow represents you and the shadow's entanglement in the grill your entanglement in life, i'll probably agree with you, the same as i'll probably agree with another to whom the same image may remind of having dropped his last token into a pavement grill, one day, when he was on 42nd Street and had to get up to the Bronx ..

*Oración a la Mano Poderosa*

*Lovedoctors and Schoolboys*

*A Threat and a Promise*

*the Exchange*

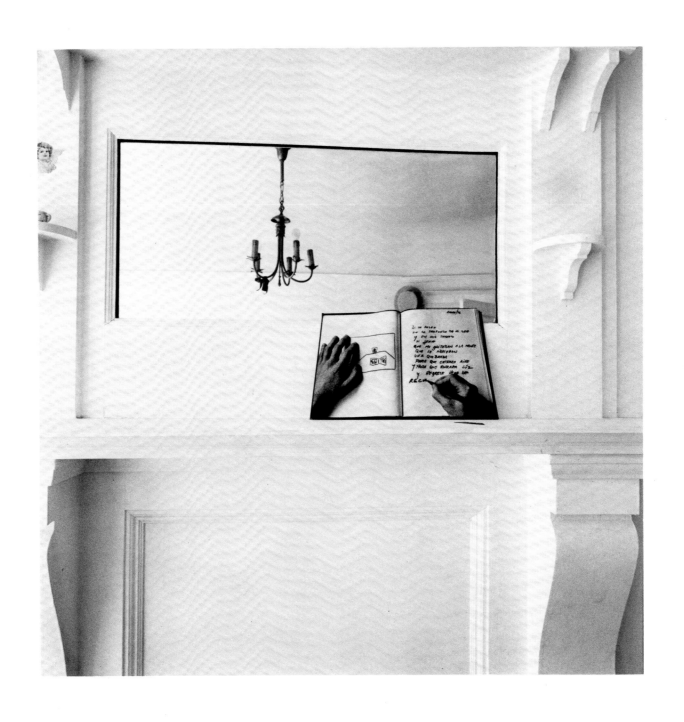

*Forgotten Memories*

Soñé que un papel caminaba
y no había viento...

*the Evidence of Things not Seen..*

en busca de un método

*Un ejercicio que repite el pasado..*

An exercise that repeats the past

*un momento retardado*

a moment delayed

un trabajo abandonado

an abandoned difficulty

*cuarto que guarda recuerdos*

divide                    guards memoire

*Rayuela*

Un problema con la Conversación

A problem with the conversation

paquete numero 825

bundle number 825

*Examining the evidence*

Memorias Olvidadas

the Logic of Limitations

*the unexpected return of the missing part..*

Sitio de Debate

*the tragic joke*

A.D. Coleman

*Jim Hughes*

*Gerard Burchard*

Ralph Gibson

Duane Michals

*Lisette Model*

André Kertész

... and as i began to disappear
i realized, someone was beginning
to forget me...

ADÁL